the longest nights

Yolanda Santa Cruz

I wish I didn't need to write these poems,
for that would mean one of two things:

a. This mess never happened.
b. It didn't affect me as much.

Both of which I'd prefer over this book.

Contents

denial

Ice trophy

He wanted to be my trophy boyfriend.

I thought trophies were meant to last forever.

I won't open your note

No letter that starts with

"I'm sorry."

can be any good.

Cyber-hopes

I dream of you
every night.
I dream that you still care.
You send videos
of when we were together.
You ask me how I'm doing.
You find ways
to say you miss me.

Perhaps, somehow,
you hacked into my dreams,
and this is your way
of letting me know
you still hurt for us.

Letting us go

I told you
I was letting us go
because it wasn't fair
to give you less
than what you could have.

I stand by it.

Still, every day,
I hope you come around
saying
I wasn't the one
who got to decide such a thing.

to tell me that you are trying.
I will fall to my knees again
when presented with your lies,
because I still want to believe
they are true.

It shouldn't matter if others have it once you don't

How do I let go of the thought
that what was once part of my life
now belongs to others
without correlating them both?

Recaps

I will reread
everything I wrote you
until my eyes can go over it
without blurring.

Until I see it clearly
and emotionless.

About us

At some point
I even stopped sharing
my poems with my friends,
for I knew
they were being
too delusional.

anger

To Gmail's twisted respect of users' preferences

I blocked his email. I wanted peace. Then, a few days ago I had to check my spam folder.

To my surprise, I found a few emails from him. I learned that day that blocking a contact just redirects the content. There is no way to stop receiving them.

Well played Gmail. Now I live in that fucking folder, hoping he will reach out, even though I don't want to.

I bet your user retention is looking pretty great.

Don't text me that you love me

Words

without

actions

are just letters

stitched together

awkwardly.

They are

hard to understand

and embarrassing

to read.

Waiting around for the one to have kids with

Disposable.
That's how I felt.

He said no.
He said
I shouldn't feel that way,
even before
I thought it was possible
for me to be such a thing.

Which made me feel
even more disposable
when I realized
I was.

I just want to walk away

I don't understand your prioritization.
I don't understand why you lie.
You don't even get sex out of it.
You don't get love.
You just get rage and blame.

Is that what you like?
Is that what gets you off?
Having people bitching at you
every step of the way?
Is that it?

What a waste of life you are
for everyone around you.
Waste of time,
of space,
of emotional bond.
I don't know why
I linger around you.
With your lack of commitment,

with your childish communication style.

You are not to blame.

It is all on me

for not walking away,

when you are crystal clear

about the way you are.

– Motherfucking song –

I've had that stupid song
stuck in my head all-day,
especially those first two lines:

"Shadows fill my mind up,
zeroes tell me my time's up."

As if
I needed to be reminded.
As if
I didn't already know.

The home we made

I built that home with you.
You had zero fucks
when you first moved in.
The only thing you got
was the bed frame.
The rest
we picked together,
then you bought it
or I brought it.
Everything in those pictures
I look up now from afar
belongs to our story.
I hope you remember that
every time you walk in.

"I wanted you in my life forever"

I wanted you too. You took that possibility out of my hands when you killed us with lies. You committed homicide on our love, as kitsch as it might sound.

Now here we are: Fucking you was as rewarding as fucking a good body that knows how to move well. You became an empty shell in front of my eyes. An object to provide momentary pleasure. You. The person I created so much bond and intimacy with.

It is what it is. I get to decide if I want to accept people for who they are, instead of who I would have liked them to be. Situations for what they are, instead of what they could have been.

Moving forward, I just want peace. I don't want to wake up thinking about your morning messages. I don't want to remember that we

once drew on Wednesdays. Not for now, at least.
Not until I process that what we had then was
real. That it wasn't part of the brush-dipped
bullshit you painted me afterwards.

After you had already changed your priorities,
but weren't brave enough to tell me a thing.

Getting close

Better to leave it here,
while I think you are still fuckable.

I don't want to get to the point
where the thought of you disgusts me.

You have read my poems

You should know better
than to push my buttons
expecting to ignite
an emotional outburst
out of my tired heart.

You should know by now
such flares are reserved
solely for my writings.
The more you do
to provoke a reaction
the more I back off
and get into them.

Back off

Stop acting like
a white man with privileges.

The privilege of putting your feelings
over everybody else's.

The privilege of ignoring
others' points of view.

Of not respecting my decision,
even though I was very clear.

The fact that you don't like it
doesn't mean it has less weight.

Our story

You had
such a great hand of cards
and handled them in a way
that would shame
even those who have never
seen a deck in their lives.

The placeholder

Truth be told,

as soon as you had the chance

to start a standard relationship

you opened your arms to it,

disregarding

everything we had built.

You changed your priorities

like a pair of shoes,

ignoring I was even your girlfriend,

ignoring that we had a commitment.

You treated me

as the leftover option

in front of freshly cut fruits.

You gave no contemplations.

Truth be told,

I was just your placeholder.

The leggings I didn't see

I don't know what I am holding on to.
It was such a shitty thing, all of it.
You were trying to fix things with me,
yet, you were giving her my birthday gift.

More than sex

Was it because she was so petite
you could fuck her standing?
Was it because
this made you feel more manly?

No, it wasn't that.
You needed your doses
of social validation,
as we all do.
This ran in abundance
hanging out with her:
The cool kid of the group.

Hurting her
meant seclusion
from the attention of the horde.
Even worse,
it meant being treated
like a traitor
from her crowd of followers.

Your fragile self-image
couldn't endure that,
so her hurt weighted
a bit more
than mine.

Sometimes you have to force chemistry
just a little bit,
just enough to believe
you are not wasting your time

Of course the nights were great.
You both always had
more Modelo in your system
than you could take out of the balcony
in three cleaning trips.
Quite the American romance,
increasing connection
by numbing the senses.
No wonder the tears
at the morning lights
at the brutal reality
of having nothing else
to bond to,
except tears and confusion.

Out of vicarious curiosity
I can't help but wonder

how you two are doing.
If the guy who never drinks
has become an alcoholic
to keep up with the game,
to be able to fuck her.
Or if reality
has succumbed to the illusion
and you are finally happy
the way we were together
with no drugs involved
since the very start.

On applied maths

You thought you would double charms
by getting a "full-time girlfriend."
I didn't want to be that,
so you ran to her.

You thought I would be the one
losing the most out of it.
Reality made sure to teach you
a good life lesson in math:
I don't care about seeing you
half of what you do.
I'm not a third as desperate,
I'm not a fifth as miserable.
Nor am I the one stuck now
with a scummily coarse partner.
I'm so fine with my choice,
happier by the day.
While by increments you notice
what you currently have
is not an eighth of us.

Bend over

I want you kneeling on the floor

looking up at me from there

until you realize

how low you would go

for someone as short as me.

Stuck

I'm so sick of it.

I'm sick of this fixated image of you,

stuck in my head day and night.

I'm sick of telling myself

that if you cared as much

you would be here.

Repeating on a loop

we accept the love

we think we deserve.

Feeling crappy

for still being open to yours.

I can't bear it any longer,

yet, every day

I drag my hopes around.

They are fifty-pound chains

that barely allow me to move.

They are worthless.

What is worse:

they are an obstacle to my freedom,

to my clarity,

to my self-love.

I hate my hopes so much.

I hate loving you.

I want to write nothing else about this,

change levels of importance,

hate me less.

I want to believe I deserve more

than the love you proved to have.

Instead,

I'm stuck missing you.

Terms and conditions

Your

"I would have given you

my whole life"

was conditional.

You would have

IF

the conditions were

just perfect

for you to do so.

IF

we were to build a life

on your terms.

I would have given it

no matter what.

No surprises

Your lies were wrapped
in translucent paper,
you believed they were hidden
while I stared at them.

I hope this burns you, because you fucking deserve it

You can.
You totally can reach out to me.
But you won't do it.

Because your pea-sized brain
is afraid of breaking the promise
you most likely made to her.
The one you probably swear
every time that she doubts you.

You are afraid of coming back
to the girl with a husband,
which would make you seem a pussy
in front of your really good,
really manly tough friends.

You are afraid of going
against your coworker's command.
The one she felt entitled to give

as soon as she learned
about me being polyamorous.

You wouldn't look too smart
coming back to me,
would you?

So yes,
you can definitely reach out,
but you won't.

Because you live in fear.
Because you live your life
out of what others think.
Because you have an ego
larger than all your wants.

This is not enough to express how I feel, but it won't ever be

I resent you.
I resent you in ways
I can't even process.
In ways I am unable to conceive,
to verbalize,
to even know I am feeling.

I resent you
for saying that you cared so much,
that you loved me like
you've never loved.
That this was a
once in a lifetime
sort of thing for you,
and then leave me waiting
day by day
for you to show up,
with my head and heart filled
with your empty words,

having to face the shallowness
of everything you wrote
day by day
realizing it was all a fallacy
driven by your needless need
to end up like a martyr,
like someone who was hurt
just as much as I was.

You didn't give a fuck.
You were the one abandoning,
leaving us for something
easier to explain
easier to keep
something more comfortable
something standard.
But you were so shady
–so fucking shady–
you wouldn't say it
in case it went wrong,
treating me
as the love of your life

on paper
while she had her shoes
already by your door,
while she wore
school girl outfits
like the ones you got me
for us to role play with.

You are disgusting.
You are heartless.
Yet,
you want to appear
as Mister Sensible.
That's what fucks me up
the most.

I resent you
on so many levels
I can't find the way
to put them together
in a stream of thoughts.

All I can say is
I don't want to see you
ever again in my life.

Erased past

How can someone go so low?

Taking down even the review he wrote about my book. As if my creativity no longer deserved his praise due to our personal fiasco. *His* fiasco. That's all he was in my life, and he proves it more by the day. A sudden hit of dopamine, meant to disappear from my existence as if it never came to be.

A dream that became a nightmare. Then I woke up and it was all done. All gone. The good and the bad. No trace of it.

I regret not jolting awake sooner. I regret sticking to the shit after I noticed the smell. Such a theft of time.

He opened these eyes of mine as few things have done. Thanks to him, I won't be falling as blindly ever again. Such a low standard, low-quality behavior. It gives me nausea at the mere thought.

Let this cross be the last one I bury. My heart can't take such insults anymore.

Points to the dictionary

Indecisive.

Insecure.

Immature.

Of course
you couldn't think
of others.
You were a walking
I.

Mortal

You will be waiting forever

for me to get back to you.

You will be damned in consumed times,

your bones grow weak and scattered,

your skin wrinkled and pale,

your eyes become empty and dull,

before I even consider

to ever get back to you.

bargaining

I won't fall for it

I am starting to play games.

I told myself

I would never play games with you.

What for?

They are worthless.

They take more energy

than what they give me in return.

They are thieves

dressed up as friends.

Their advice is cheap,

and after you have followed it

and failed,

they will turn their backs.

My store

You keep acting like a kid

that got caught stealing candy.

I keep acting as the aunt that looked away,

pretending not having seen him,

giving him another chance.

But you keep stealing,

no matter how many times

I glance over at you.

By now I should have started

treating you in accordance

with what you have proven to be.

I have failed myself in doing so.

That's why I can't forgive me,

that's why I can't move on.

Self-sabotaged healing

Dear friend of hers,
cure my heart.
Tell me he is with her.
Tell me that they are trying.
Tell me that it's working.

I just want to hear
there is no hope for me.

Let's be real

Do you think you deserve
to have your mind racing
at 1 am?

Do you think you deserve a relationship
where you feel the urge
to reach out to your phone
(the one you left in the living room
for precisely that reason)
to see if you finally got
his good night text
after 12:05 am?
Do you want that life?
Let me answer it for you:
No.
You don't.

Don't take the ruins
of what was once a coliseum
just because they are there.

I miss us

I was trying to make myself cum.
My hands were getting tired,
my pussy getting numb;
it wasn't working.

Biting my ego,
I went back to our videos.
In the first I found
I was fiercely riding you.

I heard your words.
I heard my moans.
I felt how I felt.
I was gone.

Ground-level

I lowered my standards
so it wouldn't be
as much of a step
for you to climb.
As a result
you slid over them
the way you used to do
over wet mopped floors.

Physical memory

I've moved on
but my body still lives in the same place,
and goes to the same gym,
so it's hard for her not to want
to walk with you that same path
she has many times before.
I have tried to prepare her
'cause I want her to understand
that even if you were to show up
she will have to keep moving
with only me alongside her,
the way my mind has done.

Poisoned waters

I'm so thirsty for news about you
I'd drink them from any source.

Digital Slaves

I'm as obsessed with you
as you are with me.
You check my stories
every other minute
to see if I added something new.
I check my views just as often
to see if you have watched them.

Sexual dilemma

I want to masturbate
while thinking of you,
but I think you don't deserve it
and that is a major turnoff.

God's atonement

Fucking miss him so much, dude.
Miss fucking him,
miss kissing him,
miss being drunk off his presence.
He was such a drug.

Seeing his car in my parking lot yesterday
really fucked me up.
I still want him so bad.
It's not fair to give such a narrow mind
to someone you like so much.
To someone that likes you enough
to be chasing you
three months after you cut off contact.
Like,
c'mon, God?
If I had to be mad at someone
it would be at you
for giving him such a brain
when we were so good.

depression

The longest nights

I wear a sleep mask to bed.
Every time I lift it
I pray
that it's already morning.
'Cause I have lost count
of how many times
I have woken up
still being 1 am,
and after that, 2 am.
'Cause I haven't slept
like a normal person
in about two months.
I am terrified
every time I wake up.

It was bitter

"No worries baby,

you do you."

I said over the phone

as I bit

the toffee chocolate bar

that I had bought for us.

I'm okay

What I didn't say was
I waited
for your good night message
until 11:48.

The fall

This is turning into a relationship
I don't deserve.
Or like the song goes:
"I don't know if I deserve it,
but I don't want it."

This is not what I have built.
It has taken me
a lot of effort and sacrifice
to build up this castle
for you to blow it off
like it's made of cards
while I just stare.

I don't need to see this.
I don't need you to show me
that what I thought was concrete,
solid bricks bound together
by a mortar mix,
are just cards glued at their edges

with clear egg yolk.

This is not the edification
that I thought we had.

I won't stay to see it fall.

Correlation

You promised

you would never break a promise.

You promised

you would never do

anything that hurt me.

You knew it hurt,

yet you kept going.

You broke

the most valuable thing

you could've ever given me

in the most careless,

unsympathetic way.

I can't get it back,

nor can you piece it together.

It got pulverized,

and so did my trust.

Way to set me up for misery

Every sunrise

I woke up

to his good morning messages.

Now

every sunrise

the first thought I have

is that they won't be there.

So

I write morning poems

trying to get the bitterness

of not having anything

to reply to

out of my fingers and throat.

The sketch

I keep thinking about
our planned trips.
About Tennessee,
New York,
Savannah.

So many stories drawn
in our minds
and hearts,
it's hard to accept
they were only meant
to live there.

Baguette

I'm at the Shepherd Artisan Coffee shop,
dipping a baguette into the whipped butter. It
must be around 400 calories already down.
I hold on to that piece of old, crusty bread, as if
it was my consolation prize. Because, damn, it's
been almost two weeks since we split, and I
haven't texted you since. Not even once.

Clean slate

I showed
a picture of you
to a friend today.
He looked perplexed,
unable to understand
what I saw in you.
I stared at his eyes
envious
that I'm not able
to look at it
the way he does.

Wasted

I feel so worthless

spending hours

upon hours

looking at clothes to buy.

Compulsively purchasing

whatever I don't need.

Trying to fill the void,

the emptiness,

the bareness,

the silence,

the lack of you.

Brief

It deteriorated so much. Our relationship. I don't recognize anymore what we once were. Like I only dreamed it.

I would like for you to disappear from my life. This is the point I have come to: The dream I said I wanted to live forever. Now I just want to desperately wake up.

I ask my brain to wake me from the nightmare we have become. I live terrified you will reach out, inducing me into an even deeper, ever darker stage of sleep. Harder to wake up, impossible to move, paralyzed by your presence. After all the love I felt, seems so unfair to end it in fear of you, of us, of what we've become. I would rather sleep. There, I can still dream that I trust you. That the dream is the reality and not the other way around.

This is a waking nightmare.

State

I don't want you
but I feel like
I need you so badly.
It gives me chills.
It hurts in my bones.
Gosh, I hate it here.
I can't stand knowing we exist
less than ten minutes away
and an entire life apart.

"But that makes you feel alive"

Replies the masochist
all my friends have inside
every time I explain
how it feels without you.

Too late

I need time to heal.
I need space.
Seeing messages from you
every time I look at my phone
is not giving me this.

I craved for them to arrive
for so long.
I checked my phone compulsively
every five minutes.
I wanted you to write something.
Anything.

They were never there.

Now I turn on the screen
without seeing the notifications
that I so much longed for.

Please stop.

Rainy day in Miami

Our perfect Italian village is happening on the other side of the bay. It's raining so hard there I can barely see the buildings.

I sit from afar and imagine I am there with you. That I am working from bed with you by my side, feeling your warmth. Playing soft music. The perfect day is happening, and I can just imagine it.

The buildings are completely gone by now. For a second, I wish that was always my view. To not see your building every time I sit outside.

And now it's started raining on this side as well. Fuck I miss us.

The eternal sunshine

I wish at some point

I get to forget

that you ever existed.

The way I felt with you

in our good times,

in the worst ones.

I want to leave

no trace of us.

Just like I left the apartment,

the gym,

the city.

I want to abandon

my memories

as if they were a place

I am leaving behind.

Savannah's Ghost Tour

Driving to Savannah tomorrow.

You were supposed
to be going with me.
With your new exhaust,
the one that got installed
specifically for this trip.

I will do everything we said
we would.

I will visit the cemeteries,
stay in the "Duchess" room,
take historic tours
short of the stories you knew.

I will pass the houses
I was dying to show you.
Pick up my art at the gallery.
Feel the cobblestone streets.

See the whimsical trees.

I will do everything we said
we would.

Except for the ghost tour.
As for that one, I thought
I will have plenty with yours.

Hard truth

I don't want to go to Poland
to live the experience
of being your girlfriend.
I wanted it here,
right in Miami,
right at The Yorker.
Within the home
we built together.

That won't happen
because of me.
Because what I have to offer
is not fair for you to get.
You deserve more.
We deserve more.
If I had another life,
it would have been with you.

Streets

Still waiting for the moment
when my heart stops stopping
at the sight of a blue car.

Lust, Love, and Memories' **main character asks me about this book**

I told him

I was working on my second book.

When he asked what it was about

there was a pause

in the otherwise quick replying talk.

My eyes got teary all of a sudden.

I doubted

–wasn't expecting

this dramatic mood-swing.

I wanted to say

"It's about Joe"

because he knew

the toll it took on me.

Instead,

I gulped my answer,

giving him

the generic spiel,

even though he understood

it was mainly about Joe.

June 2nd

The day I was
dying inside
writing
I would let us go
there was someone
at the *Love Life Cafe*
noting
how grateful they were
to be alive.

Delusive memories

It sucks to be writing about you now.

Now that everything is fucked up.

Now that I write out of anger,

full of resentment.

We lived so many beautiful things.

We built so much in such a short time.

I was living us.

I didn't make time to write.

Now I regret it.

Because it sucks

that when I refer to the things

I wrote about us

I won't find any of the moments we were living.

All I will see

is destruction and misery.

That's not what we were.

We were so much.

I am sorry, Love.

Tina's workout

It's soul-crushing sad to watch you

through others' stories

when we used to make our own.

I'm not

What would I give

to catch you

watching my Instagram stories

with that fake account

you think I don't know off.

That would at least mean

you are not doing so well

at getting over me.

Nightmares with you

I dreamt you biked to my place.

You were all sweaty,

physically destroyed,

looking ecstatic at the vision of me.

I saw you

and kept walking.

You found a way

to call my phone.

I answered this time.

You said you were

desperate to see me,

you couldn't take it anymore.

It weakened me

to hear your voice breaking.

I was about to walk back.

Then, you kept talking:

You said

it was a good thing I was there

because the other time you came

I wasn't.

I said:

Great for you,

starting off with another lie.

You knew I was in New York that day.

You didn't stop by.

There was no other time.

I said:

You are not a safe place for me anymore.

I don't ever want to know

anything about you.

You said you understood.

We said our goodbyes,

and

with my heart in my hands

I ended the call.

No end in sight

Depression is a bitch.
It keeps luring me back,
even when I know
I don't want what waits
on the other side of the bridge.

Still,
sadness wears me out
like her favorite outfit.
Still,
I miss the life
he wanted us to live.
Even though I know
it wouldn't have worked for me.

I keep falling and falling.
I wonder if
there will ever be an end to it.
Depression is a bitch.

Subjective time

I always wanted weekends
to be longer.
Well, they finally are,

now that you are not here.

Imagine Sundays

Weekends are the worst.
They make me second-guess.
They break me.

I start Saturday
thanking God
those nasty vibes
those shameless lies
are out of my life.
Feeling grateful
I've moved on.

By the afternoon,
I have to hold myself back
from scraping every inch of Instagram
trying to find news of him.

By evening,
I want to curl up in his arms.
I forget about how shitty it was.

At night,

I just think:

how good his life has to be now

that he never came back.

I love you too, baby

My sheets got wet this morning
with the tears I shed
right as I was coming
while I said *I love you, baby*
to an imaginary you
and he replied back.

Coming to you

Do you know
when I am coming
thinking I am with you
I cry?
How could I want
to go back to something
that even at
my imagination's peak
hurts me this bad?

Goosebumps

The more I fuck others

the more I realize

the hell of a chemistry we had.

While with them

I want to spit inside their mouths,

I want to slap them.

I wait to be choked,

to be taken from behind.

To feel the weight of their bodies,

the way I felt yours.

But they are not you,

and even when we do all this,

it feels empty, bare,

like the rehearsal of some choreography

made for two principal dancers

and given to someone else.

"'Cause you said forever, now I drive alone
past your street"

You bet
I would find the excuse
to pass by fairly often
if you didn't live
on a dead-end street.

Resemblance

The closest I've been to you in the past six years
was one hall and one seat apart in an airplane,
next to someone whose profile looked a lot like
you.

Christina's world

I just saw *Christina's world*
at the MoMA.
I almost cried with rage.
You were supposed
to be standing by my side
watching it with me
while we caressed each other.
Like one of those touchy,
sticky,
unbearably affectionate couples.

Like the one we were.

acceptance

And this is how it ends

I started writing about us
without the expectation
of sharing it with you.

Back to school

It was too cute while it lasted.
Maybe I should leave it as such,
instead of forcing more outcomes.
A memory of something sweet,
vulnerable, and fragile,
that took out the best from us.

Like a summer love.

Hollow altar figurine

I love you.

The you I thought I knew.

The one I said

there was nothing

I didn't like.

I could swear

I saw this person in you.

How did I get it so wrong?

Now I'm stuck

loving someone

that never existed,

trying to detach

the image I formed

from the body

I called you.

The break

I always said
if you want to find yourself
you should go to New York City.

I followed my advice
and broke free in the concrete
after breaking up with you.

Fade

Soon

I will even

forget

Wednesdays were

our

drawing day.

●

I started using Signal

as my messaging app

while we texted day and night.

I learned to associate

its notification icon

with our connection.

Now, I must face the fact

that it will be used

to contact everyone

but him.

I don't stalk you

Not because I'm not a creep,
but because I know it will hurt.
It hurts way too much to see you
going on with your life without me.
Even when I call myself a cerebral masochist
I'm not ready to welcome that kind of pain.

Still

I still hate you.

I would be lying to myself

if I pretended anything different.

What's worse,

I still hate myself.

I can't forgive me

for settling for old crumbs,

pretending I wasn't hungry for more.

For not having screamed.

For not going away.

I can't forgive me

for putting myself to the side

while I ran after you.

For staying awake entire nights

while your bed was already warm.

How blind I wanted to be.

I took out my eyes with spoons

and served them to you
on a silver platter.

I feel nauseated, ashamed
at how little I valued myself.
Everything I became and stopped being
to keep you in my life.
Everything I risked
without consideration.
I haven't been able
to forgive any of it.

I still hate me.

The note you shared

Was screaming not to be opened.
You didn't show up,
as you said you would.
You took away my Keep access,
so I had to request it to read it.
You didn't even send a message
letting me know you had shared it.
And it started with *"I'm sorry."*

So funny,
I just remembered
yesterday, I dreamt
that you edited it
to make it start with
"My love, ..."
The way it should have started,
regardless of what it said.

Intimacy & care

Harder, harder!
Faster, faster!
Keep going,
don't stop!

I don't need you
for any of this.
For that,
I have my vibrators
to which
I have to give
no instructions.

I wanted you
for way more than that.
For the things
I see now
you won't be able to fill.

She was so damn right

I remember that time
I showed my hairdresser
the modeling pictures
I had taken of you.
Her reply was dead-simple:
"That's not a model, dear.
That's a problem."

Clear vision

You said
you had blinders on.
Well,
I had a veil.

She helped you see
what you had around you.
She helped me see
what I had in front of me.

Facts

I was a high-risk investment.

He was into trust funds.

Scarcity mindset

I saw a dime on the floor

and I took it.

Why?

Why not?

You were giving me less

and I kept calling you.

With him

I got fried like an egg
over the roof of a car
under the Texas Sun's heat.

Jineterismo trastocado

Jamás pensé
sentir la necesidad
de amarrar a un yuma
sin querer irme de Cuba.

Peace

I finally found you
away from him.
Who would have guessed
that at some point
you would be so far
from what you once
called home.

Not going back

I can't look past the fact
you didn't care about my feelings.
Even worse,
you don't seem to realize
how much it affected me.

After all I wrote,
after all I told you,
you still think that we aren't
because of
a lifestyle disagreement.

...Although now you will know if you read this book

Yesterday was your birthday.

I didn't text,

didn't send you an email,

didn't show up,

nor left at your door

the present I bought

many moons ago.

I kept it in the folder

along with all your letters,

our drawings,

our pictures,

the necklace,

the key to what I once called home.

It was your birthday yesterday

and it hurt so much,

but you didn't deserve

to get anything from me,

not even to know

that I remembered it.

Realizations

Every day I understand more and more
I truly dodged a bullet with you.

The correction

I used to call *Love*

inconsistency,

unclarity,

low effort.

I thought that was the way

love was supposed to be.

Slowly I realized

the lie I had bought into.

The contact name got updated.

Joe had the nerve to get mad.

I almost disappeared in it

I fell into such a shitty hole with you.
I ignored all the crap
you were surrounded by
because I knew
you weren't like it.

I kept jumping right at you,
forgetting that
what keeps shit around
is most likely a sewer.

In my life

He is far from what I want
and too close to what I don't.

Not okay, but it is what it is

I need more than
what you can give.
No matter how hard you try,
you just don't know
how to treat me
the way I need
to feel appreciated and loved.
And that's fine.
I just need to understand it
and keep going
without you in my life.

Timely questions

We never finished
the *"36 questions*
to fall in love."
We were in love already.
Perhaps we will one day.
If I ever feel ready
to re-give you my love,
if you are available
to receive it then.

No drama

I mean,

he was the one who decided

to end things.

To me, we were doing good.

I told him

there was going to be

zero drama with me.

He said that's

what he was looking for.

I have got a sense that, deep down,

that's not what he wanted.

He wanted to get some drama

as a showcase of affection.

When he didn't get it

he felt unloved,

he felt unwanted.

So he left.

Hold in place

I can't move on
 –not without forgiving.
But I can't forgive you,
and I can't forgive me.

I carry this weight
as a bastaixo would
 –just that I don't want to.
There is no reward
at the end of the path.
No church being built
with the weight that I'm carrying.
It's just hindering me from looking up
when all I want is to walk straight,
when all I need is to stand tall.

No regrets

I gave my all.
I know I did.

I splayed my heart out,
showed the cuts and the blood.
I didn't hide a thing.

Life philosophy

I remember that conversation we had once. You had cut your hair short a few days before. You said you liked it long, but it just wasn't practical. With daily workouts and this Miami weather, it was taking too much time and effort to maintain. I asked you, in an ideal world, without having to worry about the weather or society, which one would be your style of preference.

It could have been punk, bald, or whatever other styles are called. You said long.

Long hair was the one you felt the best with. The one that represented you the most. Still, you decided to live without it, for very practical reasons.

And you know, babe, I can't help but see the pattern here with the way you treated us.

Reality collision

I still love you.

It doesn't matter that you don't get it.

That you are not good for me

and I'm not good for you.

That emotions aren't enough

to ignore that your vision of the world

collides with mine,

and instead of creating an expanding wave,

it limits us.

None of it seems to matter.

I still do.

I said bye while you were sleeping

Afraid and doubtful, you asked
if I preferred to pick up my stuff
instead of you dropping it by
because I wanted to feel the space
one last time
before moving on with my life
–as sort of a closure.

You were right to think
I do that kind of stuff.
What you didn't know was
that I got that already:

All the many nights
I lay next to you,
unable to sleep,
having the painful feeling
that night could be our last.

I hovered over every inch of our room

under the dim streetlights

that filtered through.

I took my glasses from the side table

and put them on

to see every detail possible.

I heard the night sounds

from the open balcony.

I was present,

I knew it was coming,

I said bye already.

Moving on

He had his seasons
and his winter was
so fucking brutal
I don't want to live
in that town anymore.

Eventually unreal

Eventually / I will start to think about you less
often / It will take me by surprise that you only
popped into my head / about four times that
month / I will feel secretly grateful /
One year will go by with me wondering /
perhaps a few times / how your life is going /
with a curiosity not strong enough / to look up
social media / My wonder will pass / as I make
in my head quick guesses about your current
situation / Then, there will come a time when I
won't even guess / I will just remember / And
someday / a few years from now / our
relationship will seem silly / Unreal even / that I
suffered so much / for someone that played me /
the way that you did.

Therapy

For every hour with you
I had to spend three
talking to my friend.

It wasn't worth it.

The deposition

He was a lawyer.
He was used to winning.

But in the trial of us
he lacked arguments,
his defense was poor,
and he lost our case.

And you keep trying so

No, babe,
you will stay blocked
'til the end of my days
because the only thing
you have proven me for sure
is that you don't deserve
to communicate with me.

Nothing more

It was your ego which kept you
compulsively checking on me.

Honesty

Be honest:

at this point you are not craving love.

Not even connection.

You are just bored

with a little too much time

on a Fourth of July.

Craving some attention,

some action to fill in the hours.

You don't fucking miss him,

and that's a relief.

Just don't lie to yourself

trying to cover up

the narcissistic appearance.

The bad dresser

was trying to measure
without marking the zones;
went too far with the scissors,
cut to the end of the fabric,
lost the rest of the roll.

You will never be welcomed

I'd be damned

if after that big of a stab

I let you get

anywhere near my back.

Bye love

I can't / I can't even be mad at your cowardice / At your lack of honesty, your absence of care / The three traits I said / I loved the most in you / Can't be upset you are not displaying them / I understand / It's hard to stay brave / when it makes you look foolish / It's hard to place bets against the odds out of love and hope / Even more having options clearly stating / you can have a comfortable life with somebody else / I can't compete with that / She knows it / You know it / And that's ok / I understand / I really do this time / Don't feel bad for me / Don't feel bad for us / Maybe one day.

Lessons

Everyone comes into your life for a reason:

to teach you something,

to lift you up,

to make you raise,

somehow.

What did he help me with?

I got to be a child again,

to be so sweet that my voice slipped out covered

in honey and cinnamon,

with sentences rolling out like melted butter.

I loved me.

I loved that delicate, innocent, vulnerable side of

me I had never seen.

I loved him.

Dearly so.

I took my heart to extents my child-self would

have been envious to see.

I cried.

As a lioness when her cub is being taken away
while she is caged and can't do anything but
roar.
I lived.
I dreamt.
I believed everything was possible with enough
will.
And it was,
as long as we all had the will to make it work.
–I was right on this one.

I also learned my lessons:
you can force no one to be part of your story.
Everyone has their own book,
even if a few chapters involve you.
I learned I am more egotistical than what I
remembered.
More than what I would like to be.
I realized some people don't deserve your
energy,
yet that won't stop you from wanting to give it.
No matter how ruthless you are,

no matter how dry you get.
You will compile, layer over layer, all the
feelings you are denying them,
carrying them everywhere you go,
as a hiking backpack that gets heavier by the
step.
The weight of its accumulation pulling you
toward earth,
until a point where it makes you bend your
knees,
falling on the ground,
unable to stand in front of all the emotions you
have carried with you for thousands of miles.
Now I know this.
I feel this heaviness every single day.

It seems like the great lesson here
is somewhere along the lines of losing my ego
and learning to let go.
I don't know where to drop that backpack
though,
if he is not there to pick it up.

I don't know how to leave my emotions by the river and walk away weightless.

How can you place all of this in a basket and turn around?

It seems like this is the ultimate lesson for me to move on.

Life can be poetic sometimes

Without even trying
we took our last selfie
at the exact same place
where we took our first one.

Autor's note

I hated writing this book. Every word of it.

I don't feel proud of what came out. It's all dark, sad, corrosive.

The worst part was editing it. Reopening every wound, making me ashamed of my thoughts, of every decision made and the way I handled things. I cried so much doing this.

But I needed to exteriorize everything I was feeling. All my emotions while losing something so dear to me. This helped me to process it. To understand that grieving is as messy as we humans are. It's never linear.

I jumped from one state to another, sometimes in a matter of minutes. It was painful. I regretted many of my words as soon as I put them on paper. Many others helped me place things into perspective, look at them objectively, keep some self-respect. All of these poems are snapshots of what I felt the very second they came out of me. I think there is power in sharing our darkest moments so others feel like they can do the same. Just like with my previous book, I wanted this one to be as sincere as I was able to be with myself.

Hopefully it will help you navigate whatever you are grieving, accepting your emotions and thoughts, knowing that you are not them: they are just states of a mind trying to make sense of a loss as well as it can.

Give yourself permission to go through all this. You will outgrow these experiences. They are not here to stay, no matter how much it seems like they are. We've got this.

Want to share your thoughts? Let's connect on Instagram @lustloveandmemories

Liked what you read? Take a peek at my debut book *Lust, Love, and Memories.*

Made in the USA
Columbia, SC
12 June 2022

61542927R00093